LAWRENCE LAWLER

Offer in Compromise for Tax Preparers

Planning for Acceptance

First edition

This book was professionally typeset on Reedsy.
Find out more at reedsy.com

All of the American, hard-working, sometimes underappreciated, tax preparers out there.

Every tax problem has a solution…

LAWRENCE M. LAWLER

Contents

Foreword

The credentials that permit a professional to represent a taxpayer before the IRS include Certified Public Accountants, Enrolled Agents, and Attorneys. Many of these are tax specialists, but very few choose to specialize in tax problem resolution services. An even larger group of tax professionals are unlicensed tax return preparers who provide tax compliance services, but are unable to provide IRS representation services to their clients. Yet, many tax return preparers are sought out by their clients when the IRS comes calling. The IRS may demand actions and payments that taxpayers cannot meet. Mr. Lawler (Larry) has authored this brief book to assist tax return preparers to appreciate how beneficial the IRS Offer in Compromise is for resolving burdensome IRS issues. He hopes this will encourage preparers to become licensed so they may offer this valuable service to clients.

After more than ten years in assisting preparers to gain tax problem resolution skills through the American Society of Tax Problem Solvers (ASTPS) educational programs I can assure you that this is achievable. Meanwhile, we continue to see the IRS and artificial intelligence chipping away at your practice base. Self-preservation should motivate you to gain the skills or partner with another professional to meet this need.

Mitchell Piper, ASTPS National Marketing Director

Preface

DISCLAIMER

To become familiar with the programs that may be employed to resolve your tax problem is a laudable and recommended investment of your time. However, reading a descriptive text on so complex a subject is not a sufficient substitute for the skills of a qualified professional who specializes in this area of practice.

Chapter 1

Introduction

An IRS Offer in Compromise (OIC) is like a financial "reset button" for taxpayers who owe more taxes than they can afford to pay. It's a chance for eligible folks to settle their tax debt for less than the total amount owed. The IRS considers their ability to pay, income, expenses, and asset equity to determine your eligibility. It's like saying, "Hey, IRS, let's make a deal!" If they accept your offer, you can get a fresh start and avoid some hefty tax burdens. It's something to consider if your client is in a tax jam!

An Offer in Compromise can help settle various federal taxes one might owe to the IRS. This includes income taxes, payroll taxes, self-employment taxes, and certain penalties and interest that have stacked up over time. It's like a one-stop shop for sorting out those tax woes and getting back on track with Uncle Sam. Just remember, not all tax types can be settled this way, but it covers a good chunk of the common ones the taxpayer might face.

It's worth noting that in some cases, an Offer in Compromise provides better relief than bankruptcy. For example, payroll taxes and trust fund recovery penalties may be settled by an OIC but may not be relieved in bankruptcy.

This book will focus on most Offers in Compromise filed by taxpayers with the IRS Collection Division. However, I will briefly overview various offers in the next chapter.

Chapter 2

Types of Offer in Compromise

T here are four types of Offers in Compromise:

- Doubt as to Collectibility
- Doubt as to Collectibility with Special Circumstances
- Effective Tax Administration
- Doubt as to Liability

Next, I'll describe each of these briefly and explain why, in this book, I will focus on just the first two OIC types.

Doubt as to Collectibility (DATC)

An IRS Doubt as to Collectibility Offer in Compromise (OIC) allows struggling taxpayers to settle their tax debt for less than the total amount they owe. The idea is pretty simple: if you can prove to the IRS that you won't be able to pay the total amount, either now or in the foreseeable future, they might agree to accept a lower payment. This allows taxpayers to get back on their feet without the burden of overwhelming tax debt.

Doubt as to Collectibility with Special Circumstances (DATCSC)

DATCSC adds an extra layer of consideration. It's similar to the regular DATC offer but considers unique situations that might not be fully captured by looking at the taxpayer's finances. These "special circumstances" could be serious health issues, a natural disaster, or other extraordinary situations that make paying their debt even harder. They are telling the IRS that even though their finances show they could pay more, they have a special reason to pay less.

So, while both types of OICs aim to help taxpayers settle their tax debt for less than they owe, the "with Special Circumstances" option provides greater flexibility, relief, and understanding for taxpayers dealing with exceptional challenges. It's like saying, "Hey, IRS, things are extra tough for me right now because of these specific reasons. Can you cut me some extra slack?"

Effective Tax Administration Offer in Compromise (ETA)

An IRS Effective Tax Administration (ETA) Offer in Compromise is a special tax settlement option designed for taxpayers who can technically pay their full tax debt. However, doing so would create an unfair or inequitable situation.

With an ETA offer, you show the IRS that while they appear to be able to pay the tax debt they owe, doing so would create significant unfairness or hardship. Upon considering their situation, the IRS might agree to settle their tax debt for less than the total amount due. An example might be when a taxpayer needs the funds to care for a disabled child. The IRS recognizes that full payment would be unjust and cause harm to the child.

It's a way for the IRS to balance the need to collect taxes with the understanding that sometimes, enforcing full payment isn't right. This option provides a fair and compassionate solution for taxpayers facing unique and challenging circumstances.

Doubt as to Liability OIC

This type of offer is for situations where you believe your taxpayer doesn't owe the total amount the IRS says they do. Maybe there's been an error, or you have new evidence that shows the tax amount assessed is incorrect. You're saying, "I don't think my client should owe this much, and here's why." If the IRS agrees that there's a genuine dispute about the amount of tax they owe, they might settle for a lower amount.

In summary, Doubt as to Liability concerns the correctness of the debt, while Doubt as to Collectibility concerns financial hardship and the inability to pay the total amount. Both provide pathways to resolve tax debt issues but address different aspects of the problem.

Going forward

From this point on, I will focus only on DATC and DATCSC, as the majority of offers a practitioner submits to the IRS Collection Division.

Although ETA OICs are also handled in the IRS Collection Division, the number of ETA OICs is minuscule compared to regular DATC or DATCSC offers. The DATL type of OIC is related to the activities of the IRS Examination Division. Therefore, I will leave the discussion of those to a future book.

Chapter 3

IRS Offer in Compromise Forms

The IRS loves its forms—they have one for almost everything! When gathering financial information, they use Collection Information Statements (CIS). There are several different forms in the CIS family, and here's a quick guide to what they are and when they're used:

- **Form 433-A (Collection Information Statement for Wage Earners and Self-Employed Individuals)**: This one is for individuals seeking Installment Agreements or Currently Not Collectible status. It's not used for Offers in Compromise (OIC).
- **Form 433-B (Collection Information Statement for Businesses)**: Similar to 433-A, but for businesses. It's used for Installment Agreements and not for OIC.
- **Form 433-A (OIC) (Collection Information Statement for Wage Earners and Self-Employed)**: Exclusively for individuals making an Offer in Compromise.
- **Form 433-B (OIC) (Collection Information Statement for Businesses)**: Exclusively for businesses making an Offer in Compromise.

- **Form 433-F (Collection Information Statement)**: This form collects financial info from individuals or businesses to assess their ability to pay tax debts. It's often called the "Short Form 433-A."
- **Form 433-D (Installment Agreement)**: This is the agreement between the IRS and a taxpayer to set up a payment plan for outstanding tax debt.
- **Form 656 (Offer in Compromise)**: This is the official agreement where the IRS agrees to accept a reduced amount to settle a taxpayer's total debt. It usually comes with Form 433-A (OIC).
- **Form 656-L (Offer in Compromise - Doubt as to Liability)**: This form is for when there's a dispute about the amount of tax owed, and the IRS agrees to settle for a lower amount.

All these forms can get pretty confusing with their similar names and numbers! To keep things simple, in this book, we'll focus only on the forms you need for Doubt as to Collectibility (DATC) or Doubt as to Collectibility with Special Circumstances (DATCSC). So, we'll discuss forms 433-A (OIC), 433-B (OIC), and 656 from the list above.

Fillable forms may be found on the IRS website IRS.gov.

Chapter 4

Essential Offer in Compromise Elements

Equity Component - What Does Your Taxpayer Own and Owe?

Let's talk about the equity component of an IRS Offer in Compromise. This is a big part of determining taxpayers' ability to settle their debt. Here's what you need to know:

1. **Equity Basics:** Equity is the value of an asset after subtracting any debts against it. For example, if a taxpayer owns a house worth $200,000 and still owes $150,000 on the mortgage, the equity in the house is $50,000. Simple, right?

2. **Why Equity Matters:** The IRS uses equity to determine how much taxpayers can pay for their debt. They look at the total equity in all assets, such as homes, cars, and investments. If a taxpayer has a lot of equity, the IRS might expect a larger payment. But if their equity is low, the offer amount might be lower, too.

3. **Calculating Equity:** To figure out equity, we:

- Look at the current fair market value (FMV) of each asset.
- Subtract any loans or liens tied to those assets. For instance, if a taxpayer's car is worth $10,000 and owes $6,000, the equity is $4,000.

1. **Impact on the Offer:** Equity helps the IRS decide whether to accept the offer and for how much. If the taxpayer's total equity exceeds the tax debt, they'll likely need to offer more. If it's less, they can offer a lower amount.

2. **Special Considerations:** Sometimes, there are special circumstances like high medical bills or severe economic hardship. The IRS might take these into account and be more flexible about equity. They understand that selling assets might not always be practical or fair, especially if it impacts the taxpayer's well-being.

- Example: A taxpayer with significant home equity may be unable to borrow against the equity due to tax debt or weak creditworthiness. Therefore, the taxpayer must sell the home to access the equity. However, if the taxpayer cannot afford to live elsewhere for less than his present home or if he cannot afford the cost to move, then the equity isn't accessible without incurring undue economic hardship.

The equity component involves assessing what the taxpayer owns versus what they owe and using that information to determine a fair offer. By accurately presenting a taxpayer's equity, we can help the IRS understand their financial situation and work towards settling the debt in a manageable way.

Got it? Great! Let's move on to the Income Component.

Income Component - What Does Your Client Earn Compared to Their Expenses?

Now, let's dive into the Income Component of an IRS Offer in Compromise. This is another crucial puzzle piece when evaluating taxpayers' ability to settle their debt. Here's what you need to understand:

1. **Income Overview:** The IRS looks at a taxpayer's gross income to see how much money is coming in regularly. This includes wages, salaries, self-employment income, rental income, interest, dividends, and even things like alimony or child support. Essentially, it's all sources of cash flowing to the taxpayer - before taxes.
2. **Why Income Matters:** Income is key because it shows the IRS how much taxpayers can realistically afford to pay monthly. Higher income usually means the IRS will expect a higher payment, while lower income can help justify a lower offer amount.
3. **Evaluating Income:** To evaluate income, we need:

- Pay stubs or wage statements.
- Profit and loss statements for self-employed individuals.
- Bank statements showing deposits.
- Documentation of additional income sources, like rental agreements or investment statements. Analyzing this information gives us a clear picture of the taxpayer's financial inflow.

1. **Disposable Income:** One of the key things the IRS looks at is disposable income. This is the income left after necessary living expenses are paid. Necessary expenses include housing, utilities, food, transportation, and healthcare. The more disposable income a taxpayer has, the more the IRS will expect them to pay towards their tax debt. IRS has standards that limit the amount of expenses they deem allowable; therefore, a taxpayer living a lavish lifestyle will find their allowable expenses limited.

The IRS calls excess income the amount by which monthly income exceeds monthly expenses. This is the base figure the IRS employs when computing future income. If a taxpayer can pay the offered amount in five or fewer months, the IRS will allow the taxpayer to count only twelve months of the *excess income*. If taxpayers need more time to pay, they can have up to twenty-four months. Therefore, when a taxpayer needs more than five months to pay, the IRS will use twenty-four months of *excess income*. Thus, the Future Income Component is either twelve or twenty-four months of *excess income*.

1. **Impact on the Offer:** The IRS uses income to assess taxpayers' ability to make monthly payments. If a taxpayer has a high income but low expenses, they might need to offer more, or the IRS may reject the offer in favor of an Installment Agreement. Conversely, the IRS may accept a lower offer if their income barely covers their

essential expenses.

2. **Special Considerations:** Just like with equity, special circumstances can affect how income is viewed. For example, if a taxpayer recently lost their job or has variable income due to seasonal work, the IRS might consider these factors when evaluating the offer.

3. **Critical Step:** Tax professionals preparing OICs must multiply the monthly payments a taxpayer could make times the number of months remaining until the Collection Statute Expiration Date (CSED). If that amount is significantly greater than the offer amount, the IRS will likely reject the offer and suggest an Installment Arrangement.

So, the income component is about understanding the taxpayer's cash flow and what they can reasonably pay each month after covering their necessary expenses. By accurately presenting this information, practitioners help the IRS understand the taxpayer's financial situation, making it easier to reach a fair agreement.

Got it? Awesome! Now, let's get into how the IRS uses the Equity and Income Components to determine what they believe to be the taxpayer's Reasonable Collection Potential (RCP).

What Does IRS Mean By Reasonable Collection Potential?

Let's consider the IRS term "Reasonable Collection Potential, or RCP." The IRS uses this key concept to decide whether to accept an Offer in Compromise. Here's what you need to know:

1. **What is RCP?** Reasonable Collection Potential is the IRS's estimate of how much money they can reasonably expect to collect from a taxpayer, both now and in the future. It combines the taxpayer's net realizable equity in assets and their future income

after necessary living expenses.

2. **Why RCP Matters:** RCP is important because it sets the baseline for what the IRS will consider an acceptable offer. If your offer exceeds your RCP, the IRS is more likely to accept it. If it's below, they'll probably reject it.

3. **Components of RCP:** RCP has two main components:

- **Equity in Assets:** This is the value of what the taxpayer owns (like a home or car) minus what they owe on those assets. We already talked about this part.
- **Future Income:** After accounting for necessary living expenses, the taxpayer's projected income. We also covered this.

1. **Calculating RCP:** To calculate RCP, the IRS looks at:

- The total equity in the taxpayer's assets.
- The taxpayer's disposable income over a set period (usually 12 to 24 months). For example, if a taxpayer has $50,000 in equity and a monthly disposable income of $500, their RCP might be $50,000 + ($500 x 12 months) = $56,000.

1. **Impact on the Offer:** The IRS evaluates the offer amount using RCP. If the taxpayer's offer exceeds their RCP, the IRS will likely expect a higher offer. If it's at or above the RCP, the offer has a good chance of acceptance.

2. **Special Considerations:** Sometimes, special circumstances can influence RCP. For instance, the IRS might adjust its expectations if a taxpayer has significant medical expenses or other hardships. The idea is to be fair and reasonable, considering taxpayers' ability to pay without causing undue hardship.

So, Reasonable Collection Potential is all about figuring out the maximum amount the IRS thinks they can collect based on the taxpayer's assets and future income. By accurately calculating and presenting RCP, we can help the IRS understand the taxpayer's situation and work towards a fair settlement.

Got it? Great! Now, let's review how we gather and document the information needed to calculate RCP accurately.

Chapter 5

Determining Equity Component Values

When working on an Offer in Compromise, the IRS looks at the value of taxpayers' assets and any encumbrances against them. Here's how they do it:

1. **Valuing Assets:** The IRS wants to know the fair market value of each taxpayer's asset. This includes things like:

- **Real Estate:** The current market value of homes, rental properties, and land.
- **Vehicles:** The value of cars, trucks, motorcycles, boats, and RVs.
- **Bank Accounts:** The checking, savings, and other financial accounts balances.
- **Investments:** The value of stocks, bonds, retirement accounts, and other investments.
- **Personal Property:** The value of valuable personal items like jewelry, collectibles, and artwork.

1. To determine these values, taxpayers might need to provide:

- Recent appraisals or market analyses for real estate.
- Kelley Blue Book or similar valuations for vehicles.
- Recent bank and investment account statements.

1. **Considering Encumbrances:** Encumbrances are any debts or liens against these assets. The IRS subtracts these from the asset's value to determine the equity. For example:

- **Mortgages:** The remaining balance on a home loan.
- **Car Loans:** The amount still owed on a vehicle.
- **Liens:** Any other legal claims against the asset, like a tax lien.

1. **Calculating Net Equity:** Net equity is the asset's value minus encumbrances. This gives the IRS a clear picture of what the taxpayer owns, which is free and clear. Here's how it works:

- **House Example:** Value = $200,000, Mortgage = $150,000, Net Equity = $50,000.
- **Car Example:** Value = $10,000, Car Loan = $6,000, Net Equity = $4,000.

1. **Why This Matters for an OIC:** The IRS uses this net equity to help calculate the taxpayer's Reasonable Collection Potential (RCP). If taxpayers have significant equity in their assets, the IRS might expect them to use it to pay down their tax debt. If the equity is low, it can justify a lower offer amount.
2. **Documentation:** Taxpayers must provide documentation to support the values and encumbrances of their assets. This might include appraisal reports, loan statements, and account summaries.

Best Practice Recommendation: Use the IRS Form 433-A (OIC) as a checklist to find planning opportunities. First, enter all the data as provided by your client. Next, examine each item entered to consider any actions you could recommend to make the offer more likely to be accepted or reduce the amount offered. For example, if a taxpayer has a significant balance in a savings account, he might pay down his auto loan or mortgage principal. The payment reduces the cash asset but may not change the asset value of the auto or the home to be counted in the offer.

After reviewing entries on the form, look at the areas without entries to determine if you can recommend actions that could be entered and make the offer better for the taxpayer. For example, if the taxpayer has no entry for health or life insurance, you could recommend securing them. The monthly payment would reduce the net income as they are allowable expenses. The offer calculation is based on a multiple of net income, which would reduce the offer amount by either twelve or twenty-four times the added monthly insurance expense.

The taxpayer must be paying the new expenses when the offer is submitted. Although continuing health and life insurance is prudent for taxpayers' well-being, they could cease having it after the offer is finalized.

So, in summary, the IRS values assets by examining their fair market value and subtracting any encumbrances to determine their net equity. This net equity is crucial to assessing how much the taxpayer can afford to pay in an Offer in Compromise.

Let's move on to how we might affect an OIC's equity amount.

Equity Planning to Reduce the Amount of an OIC

Let's look at how a tax professional can use equity planning tips and techniques to potentially reduce the amount of an Offer in Compromise (OIC). This is all about strategically presenting the taxpayer's financial situation to make the offer more acceptable to the IRS. Here are some examples:

1. **Documenting Lower Asset Values:**

- **Real Estate:** Obtain a current market analysis or appraisal showing a lower value than what might be listed on online sites the IRS employs. Highlight any factors that could lower the value, such as needed repairs or market downturns.
- **Vehicles:** Use trade-in rather than retail values from sources like Kelley Blue Book. Document any damage or high mileage that reduces the vehicle's worth.

1. **Highlighting Encumbrances:**

- **Mortgages and Loans:** Ensure all outstanding mortgage balances and other liens are accurately documented and deducted from the asset's value. This reduces the net equity.
- **Property Tax Arrearages:** Reduce asset value and may impede the sale of said property.
- **Personal Loans:** Document personal loans or lines of credit secured by the taxpayer's assets, reducing the available equity.

1. **Exempt Assets:**

- **Retirement Accounts:** In some cases, certain retirement accounts (like IRAs and 401(k)s) may be discounted, especially if the taxpayer is of retirement age or may be relying on them to meet necessary living expenses—generally, the IRS levies such accounts as a last-ditch option.
- **Household Goods and Personal Effects:** These are usually

exempt up to a certain value. Ensure that normal household items are valued conservatively and excluded from equity.

1. **Strategic Use of Cash:**

- **Paying Down Debts:** Advise the taxpayer to use available cash to pay down secured debts, which can reduce equity. For instance, paying down a car loan can reduce the equity in bank accounts without increasing the equity in the vehicle.
- **Necessary Living Expenses:** Make sure the taxpayer uses cash for necessary expenses rather than accumulating it by living below normal standards. This can lower the available funds the IRS might expect them to use for the offer.

1. **Leveraging Future Income Projections:**

- **Variable Income:** If the taxpayer has a fluctuating income, document periods of lower income to present a realistic average. This can reduce the disposable income calculation.
- **Upcoming Financial Changes:** If the taxpayer expects a reduction in income due to retirement, health issues, or other factors, document these changes to show a lower future income.

1. **Medical and Hardship Considerations:**

- **Medical Expenses:** Highlight anticipated medical expenses and provide credible documentation to support these expenses, such as doctor's letters.
- **Hardship Situations:** Document any special circumstances, such as caring for an elderly parent or a disabled child, which increase necessary expenses and reduce the ability to pay. For example,

consider the expense of making a home handicapped-accessible or the expectation of in-home living assistance.

1. **Asset Transfers:**

- **Gifting Assets:** If appropriate and done well before filing the OIC, advise on legally permissible asset transfers to family members. Be cautious, as the IRS looks at recent transfers and can reverse them if done to evade taxes.
- **Trusts:** In some cases, placing assets in a trust can be a strategic move, though this requires careful planning and compliance with legal standards. The IRS may ultimately consider trust assets to belong to the taxpayer.

By employing these equity planning tips and techniques, a tax professional can help present the taxpayer's financial situation in a way that maximizes the chances of the IRS accepting a lower Offer in Compromise. The goal is to accurately and strategically document all factors that reduce the taxpayer's net equity and disposable income, making a compelling case for a lower settlement amount.

Chapter 6

Income Component Elements

Income Planning to Reduce the Amount of an OIC

N
ow, let's review some income planning tips and techniques a tax professional might use to help reduce the amount of an Offer in Compromise (OIC). These strategies aim to accurately present the taxpayer's financial situation to show a lower ability to pay. Here are some examples:

1. **Accurate Income Documentation:**

- **Variable Income:** For taxpayers with fluctuating income, use a longer period to calculate the average income, especially if recent months show lower earnings. Document any seasonal or temporary drops in income.
- **Business Expenses:** Document all legitimate business expenses to reduce reported net income. This includes supplies, equipment, and other deductible expenses.

1. **Future Income Changes:**

- **Imminent Retirement:** If the taxpayer is close to retirement, document the expected reduction in income due to the shift from wages to retirement benefits, which are often lower.
- **Health Issues:** Document any health issues that might reduce work hours or earnings. Provide medical records and doctor's notes as evidence.

1. **Living Expense Adjustments:**

- **Actual Living Expenses:** Ensure the IRS considers all allowable living expenses. Provide detailed documentation for rent, utilities, food, healthcare, and transportation expenses.
- **High Necessary Expenses:** Highlight and document any unusually high necessary expenses, such as high medical costs or care for dependents with special needs, which can reduce disposable income.

1. **Income Exclusions:**

- **Non-recurring Income:** If the taxpayer recently received a one-time payment (like a bonus or settlement), document it as non-recurring to avoid it being considered as part of regular income.
- **Family Gifts and Support:** A financially challenged taxpayer may sometimes receive funds and other support from family. Beware that the IRS will include regular support and assistance in the positive cash flow, increasing the offer amount. It is best to curtail such practices, which generally cannot be maintained regardless.

1. **Spousal Income:**

- **Separate Finances:** If applicable, document separate finances for spouses. The IRS might only consider the taxpayer's income, not the spouse's if they maintain separate finances. Spousal income may require a pro-rata allocation of living expenses as the liable taxpayer does not pay all the living expenses. The IRS presumes each household income stream supports necessary expenses proportionately.

- **Marital Status Changes:** If the taxpayer is recently separated or divorced, ensure this change is documented, and the spouse's income is excluded from the calculation.

1. **Business Income Considerations:**

- **Depreciation and Amortization:** The IRS will add back depreciation and amortization for self-employed taxpayers as they are expenses that do not require cash.
- **Business Debt Payments:** Document all business debt payments to show they reduce disposable income. Business expenses generally include interest but not principal reduction. For offer purposes, this should be used to reduce cash flow to the household.

1. **Anticipated Reductions:**

- **Contract Endings:** If the taxpayer's contract job is ending or they expect a layoff, document these anticipated income reductions.
- **Economic Downturns:** If the taxpayer's industry is experiencing a downturn, provide evidence of reduced business or employment opportunities.

1. **Review and Adjust Current Income:**

- **Optimize Deductions:** Ensure taxpayers take advantage of all allowable deductions and credits to reduce taxable income. For example, a taxpayer may drive an old vehicle with no monthly auto or lease payment, which would be an allowable expense for offer purposes. It may be prudent to secure a safer and more reliable vehicle with the accompanying allowable expense, reducing the offer amount. The net effect may be that the auto payment has reduced the required offer to the point that the net cost to the taxpayer is zero.

- **Expense Tracking:** Advise taxpayers to diligently track all allowable expenses to provide a complete and accurate picture of their financial situation.

By implementing these income planning concepts, a tax professional can help present a taxpayer's financial situation in a way that accurately reflects their true ability to pay. Often, this advice corrects prior bad financial decisions and, in turn, aids in achieving an acceptable OIC. The key is thorough documentation, strategic presentation, and better financial behavior.

Chapter 7

Conclusion

L et's wrap up this excursion into Offers in Compromise by highlighting the importance of documentation, other factors the IRS considers, and the advantages and disadvantages of an OIC.

Importance of Documentation in a Successful Offer:

1. **Accuracy and Transparency:**

- Providing thorough and accurate documentation is crucial. This includes proof of income, expenses, asset values, and encumbrances. Accurate documentation ensures the IRS has a clear and honest picture of the taxpayer's financial situation.

1. **Supporting Claims:**

- Proper documentation supports the claims made in the OIC application. Solid evidence strengthens the case, whether about the value of assets, the amount of income, or the extent of necessary expenses.

1. **Demonstrating Financial Hardship:**

* Documenting financial hardships is essential to justifying a lower offer. Examples include medical bills, employment termination notices, or proof of dependents' needs.

Other Factors the IRS Considers:

1. **Age:**

* The taxpayer's age can impact their ability to work and generate income. Older taxpayers, especially those close to retirement, might have reduced earning potential or imminent needs for retirement funds.
* Younger taxpayers have more earning years, during which they may increase their ability to pay the total amount they owe. This may diminish the IRS's inclination to accept a reduced amount.

1. **Health:**

* Health issues can significantly affect taxpayers' ability to work and incur additional expenses. Medical records and doctor's statements can provide evidence of these challenges.

1. **Occupation and Employment:**

* The nature of the taxpayer's job, job stability, and future employment prospects are important. The IRS considers whether the taxpayer's occupation has a high or low earning potential.

1. **Dependents:**

- The number of dependents and their needs affect the taxpayer's disposable income. Documentation of dependents' expenses, such as childcare, education, and healthcare, is important.

Advantages of an OIC:

1. **Debt Relief:**

- Negotiating an OIC can significantly reduce the taxpayer's total tax debt, providing financial relief and a fresh start.

1. **Avoiding Bankruptcy:**

- An OIC can be a preferable alternative to declaring bankruptcy, which negatively impacts credit and financial standing.
- Payroll taxes and trust fund recovery penalties can be compromised; they cannot be discharged in bankruptcy.

1. **Stopping Collection Actions:**

- Once an OIC is processable, the IRS will halt enforced collection actions, including levies and garnishments.

1. **Resolving Tax Issues:**

- An OIC can resolve outstanding tax liabilities, reducing stress and uncertainty for the taxpayer.

Disadvantages of an OIC:

1. **Strict Eligibility Requirements:**

- Not all taxpayers qualify for an OIC. The IRS has strict guidelines and criteria that must be met, which can be challenging.

1. **Lengthy Process:**

- The OIC process can be time-consuming, taking several months to complete.

1. **Disclosure of Financial Information:**

- Taxpayers must provide detailed financial information, which can feel invasive and requires careful preparation.

1. **Compliance Requirement:**

- Taxpayers must pay the offer amount within the agreed period, generally five months, or for a higher amount within twenty-four months.
- Taxpayers must comply with all filing and payment requirements for five years after the OIC is accepted. Failure to do so can result in the reinstatement of the original debt.

Conclusion:

A successful Offer in Compromise hinges on meticulous documentation, demonstrating the taxpayer's inability to pay the full tax debt. The IRS also considers various personal factors such as age, health, occupation, employment status, and dependents, which can influence the outcome. Understanding the advantages and disadvantages of an OIC helps taxpayers make informed decisions about seeking this form of tax relief.

About the Author

Okay, that may not be my picture. However, it is my Buddy. I'll tell you a little about me. I have been a practicing CPA and Enrolled Agent for over 50 years. As Managing Partner of Lawler & Witkowski, CPAs, PC, I have been afforded the luxury of making most of the mistakes a small firm owner can make. The one opportunity not missed was commencing to offer tax problem resolution services and from that launching the American Society of Tax Problem Solvers.

I hope this short book might aid you to see the same opportunity and encourage you to investigate further. Go to ASTPS.org and explore for yourself. Opportunity may only knock once, be sure you are listening for its sound.

Also by Lawrence Lawler

Solve Your Tax Problem, Now. Grow Your Practice with Newsletter Marketing Lies, Myths, and Misconceptions About the IRS The Truck Driver's Guide to IRS Audits

www.ingramcontent.com/pod-product-compliance
Lightning Source LLC
Chambersburg PA
CBHW072005210526

45479CB00003B/1074